HAL•LEONARD®

Piano Play-Along

PIANO | VOCAL | GUITAR • AUDIO   **VOLUME 73**

AUDIO ACCESS INCLUDED

PLAYBACK+
Speed • Pitch • Balance • Loop

MAMMA MIA!™

THE MOVIE SOUNDTRACK FEATURING THE SONGS OF ABBA®

T0057745

To access audio visit:
www.halleonard.com/mylibrary

6118-1143-6900-4952

ISBN 978-1-4234-6687-1

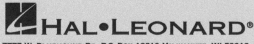

HAL•LEONARD®
7777 W. BLUEMOUND RD. P.O. BOX 13819 MILWAUKEE, WI 53213

Visit Hal Leonard Online at
www.halleonard.com

CONTENTS

PAGE TITLE

DANCING QUEEN

Words and Music by BENNY ANDERSSON,
BJÖRN ULVAEUS and STIG ANDERSON

Strong Rock

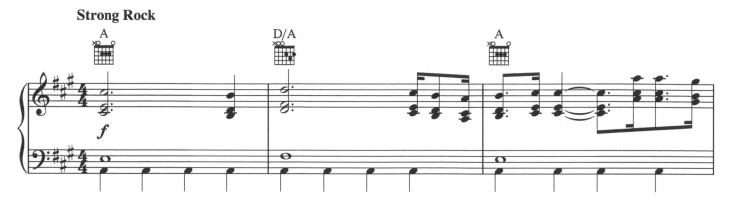

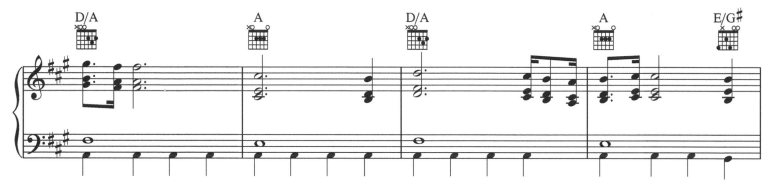

You can dance. __ You can jive, _____

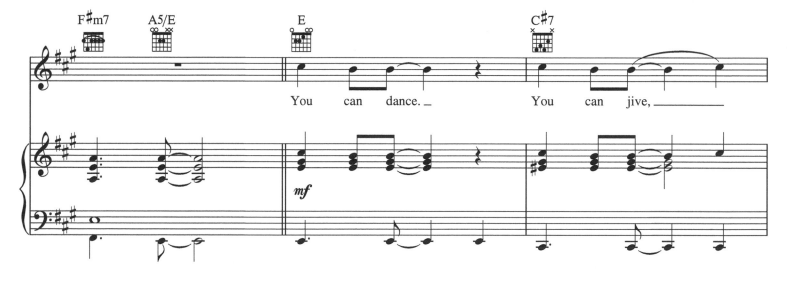

hav- ing __ the time of __ your life. __ Oh, _____ see that __ girl. __

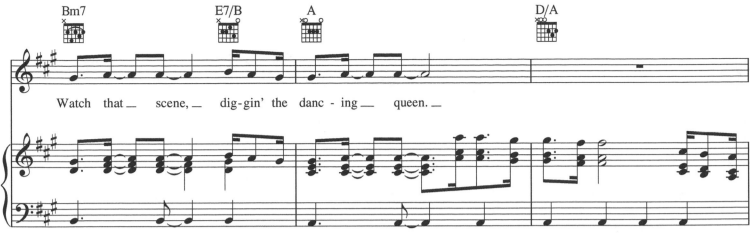

Watch that __ scene, __ dig-gin' the danc - ing __ queen. __

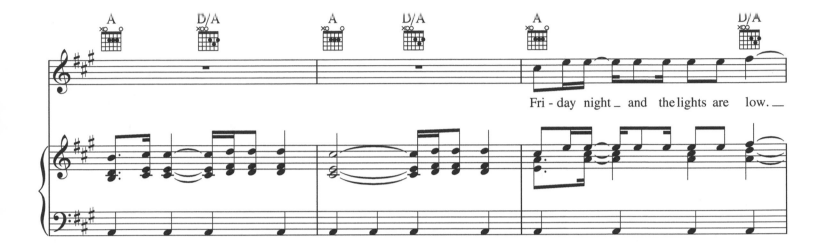

Fri - day night __ and the lights are low. __

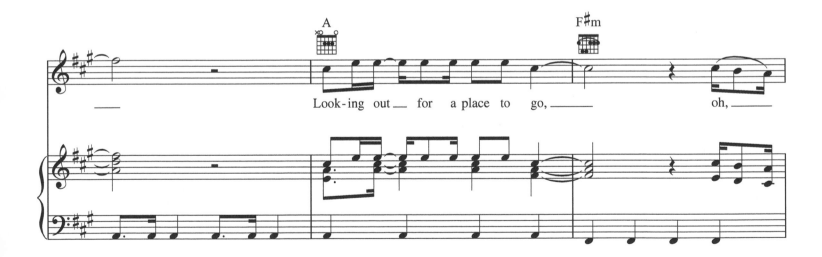

__ Look-ing out __ for a place to go, _____ oh, _____

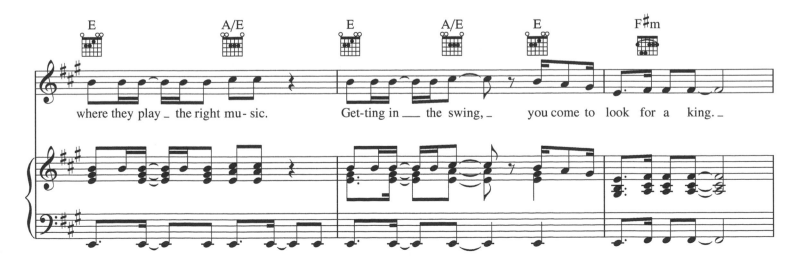

where they play __ the right mu - sic. Get-ting in ___ the swing, __ you come to look for a king. __

young and_ sweet,_ on-ly sev-en-teen._

Danc-ing_ queen,_ feel the_ beat_ from the tam-bou-rine._

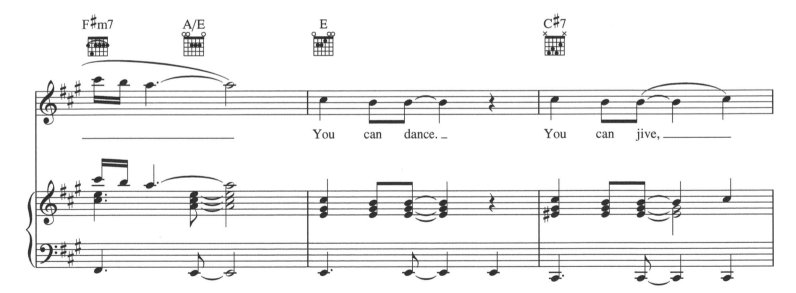

_ You can dance._ You can jive,_

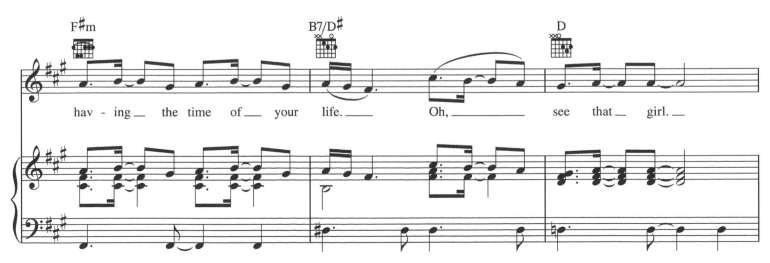

hav-ing_ the time of_ your life._ Oh,_ see that_ girl._

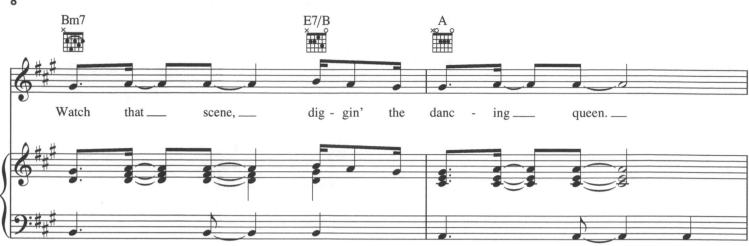

Watch that ___ scene, ___ dig-gin' the danc-ing ___ queen.

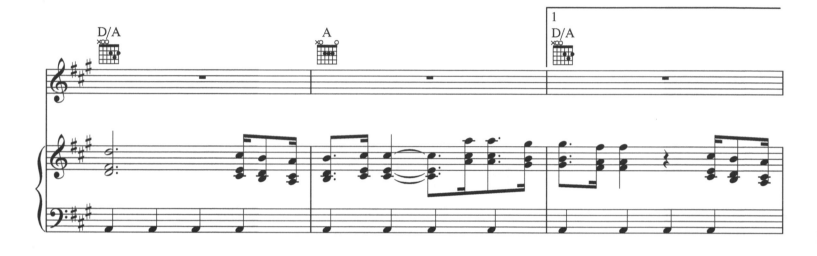

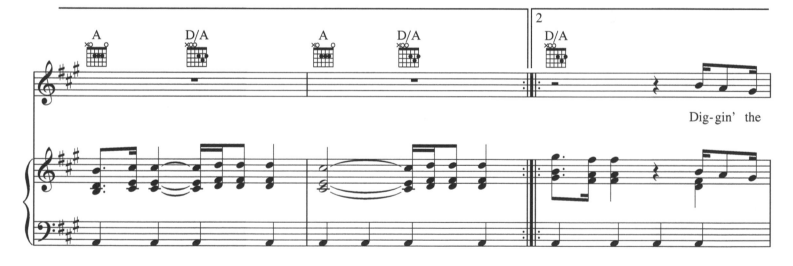

Dig-gin' the

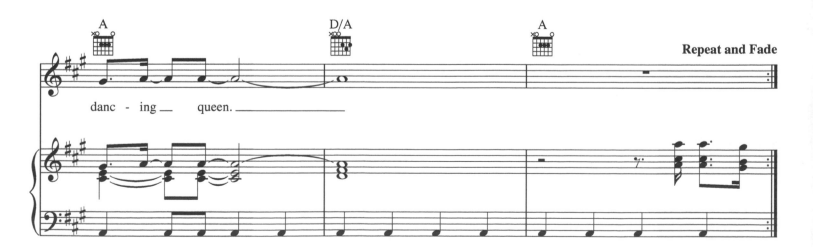

Repeat and Fade

danc - ing ___ queen. _____

GIMME! GIMME! GIMME!
(A Man After Midnight)

Words and Music by BENNY ANDERSSON
and BJÖRN ULVAEUS

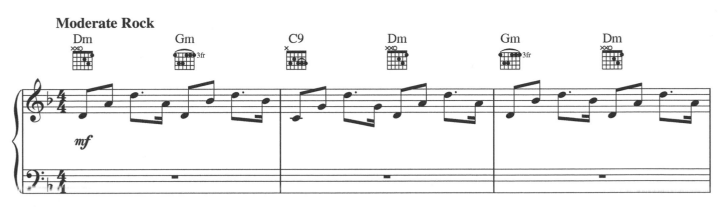

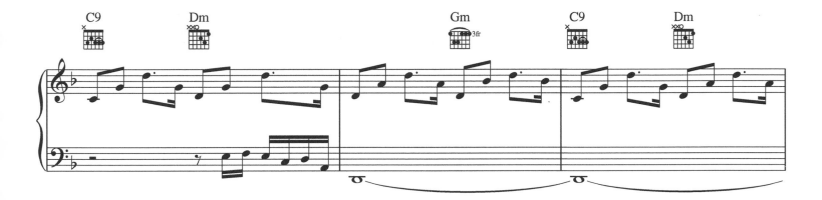

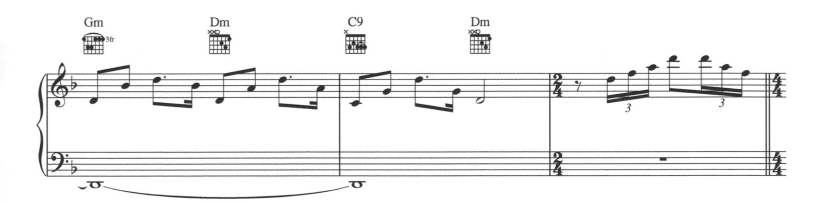

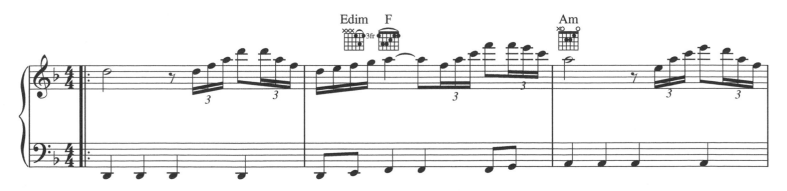

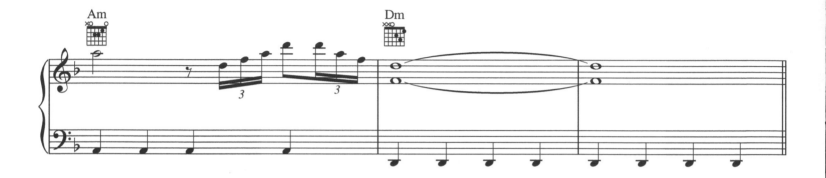

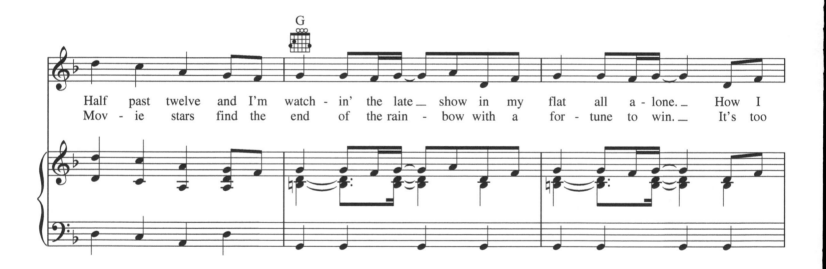

Half past twelve and I'm watch-in' the late _ show in my flat all a - lone. _ How I
Mov - ie stars find the end of the rain - bow with a for - tune to win. _ It's too

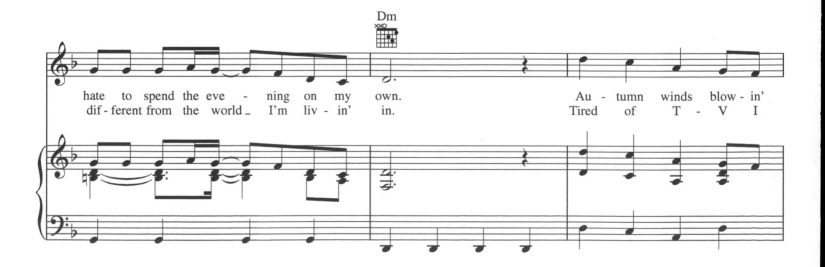

hate to spend the eve - ning on my own. Au - tumn winds blow - in'
dif - ferent from the world _ I'm liv - in' in. Tired of T - V I

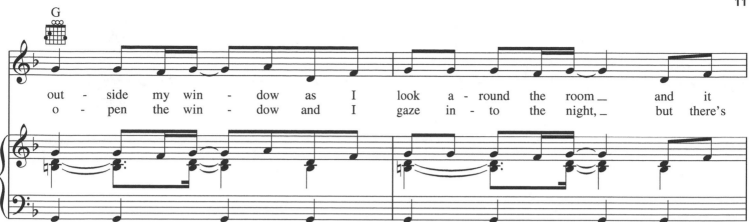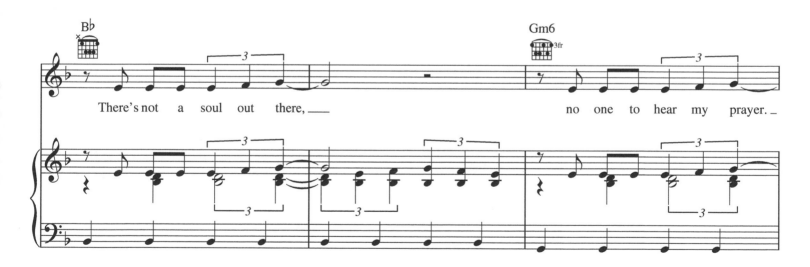

Gim-me! Gim-me! Gim-me! a man____ af-ter mid - night. Won't___ some-bod-y help me chase the

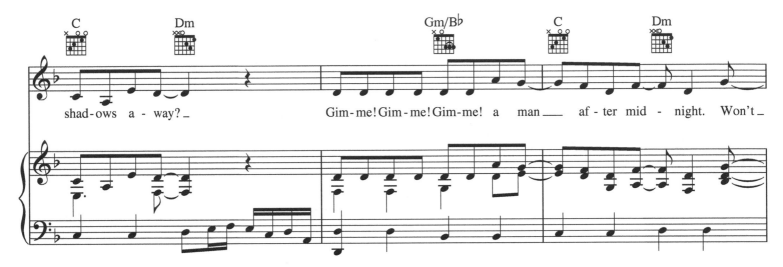

shad-ows a - way?____ Gim-me! Gim-me! Gim-me! a man____ af-ter mid - night. Won't___

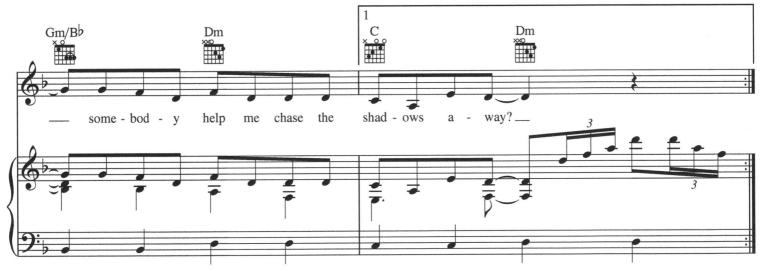

____ some-bod-y help me chase the shad-ows a - way?____

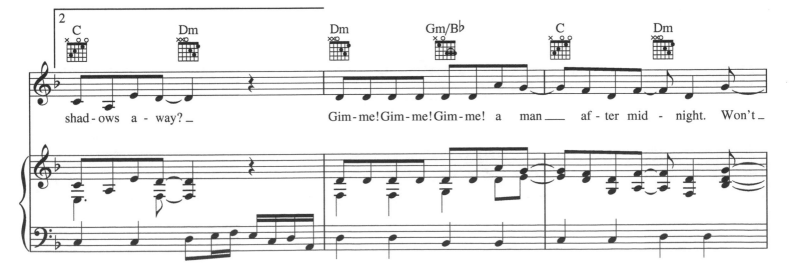

shad-ows a - way?____ Gim-me! Gim-me! Gim-me! a man____ af-ter mid - night. Won't____

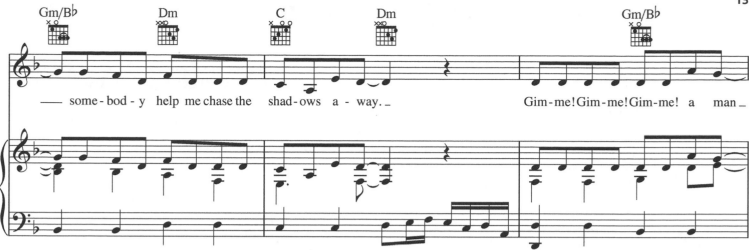

some - bod - y help me chase the shad - ows a - way. Gim-me! Gim-me! Gim-me! a man

af - ter mid - night, take me through the dark-ness to the break of the day.

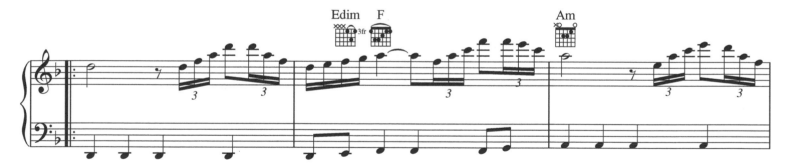

Repeat and Fade

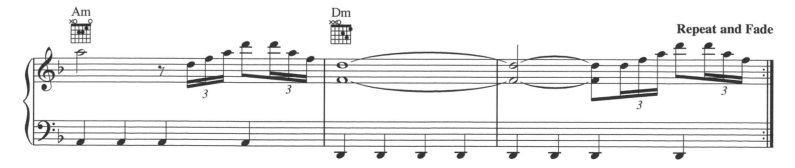

HONEY, HONEY

Words and Music by BENNY ANDERSSON,
BJÖRN ULVAEUS and STIG ANDERSON

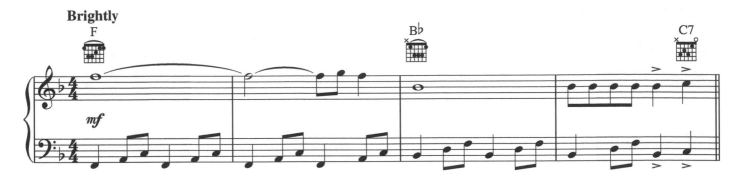

Hon-ey, hon-ey, how you thrill me, a-ha, hon-ey, hon-ey.
Hon-ey, hon-ey, let me feel it, a-ha, hon-ey, hon-ey.
Hon-ey, hon-ey, touch me, ba-by, a-ha, hon-ey, hon-ey.

Hon-ey, hon-ey, near-ly kill me, a-
Hon-ey, hon-ey, don't con-ceal it, a-
Hon-ey, hon-ey, hold me, ba-by, a-

ha, hon-ey, hon-ey.   I'd heard a-bout you be-fore,
ha, hon-ey, hon-ey.   The way that you kiss good-night,
ha, hon-ey, hon-ey.   You look like a mov-ie star,

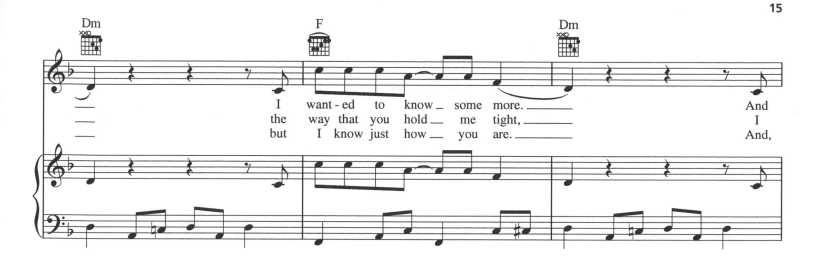

I want-ed to know some more. And
the way that you hold me tight, I
but I know just how you are. And,

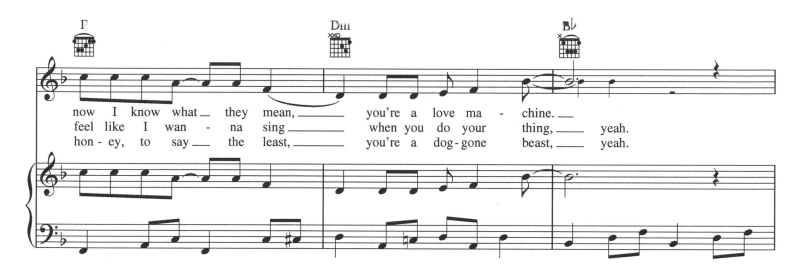

now I know what they mean, you're a love ma - chine.
feel like I wan - na sing when you do your thing, yeah.
hon - ey, to say the least, you're a dog - gone beast, yeah.

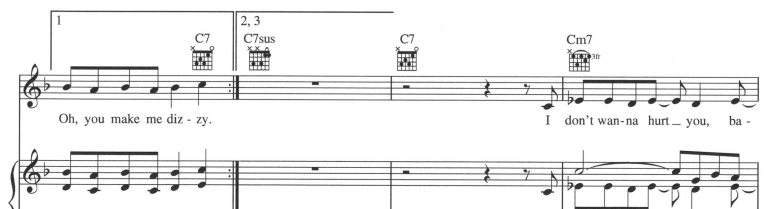

Oh, you make me diz - zy.
I don't wan - na hurt you, ba -

- by, I don't wan - na see you cry. So stay on the ground, girl, you

bet-ter not get too high. ___ But I'm gon-na stick to you, ___

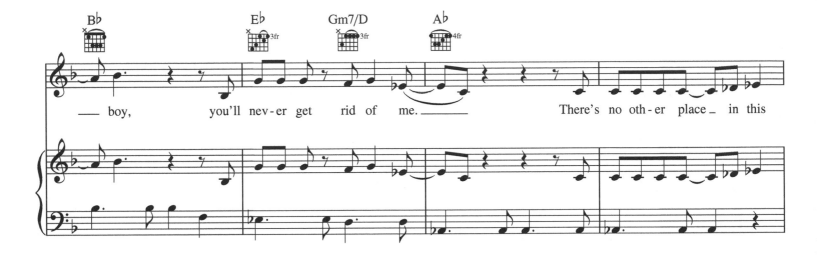

___ boy, you'll nev-er get rid of me. _____ There's no oth-er place ___ in this

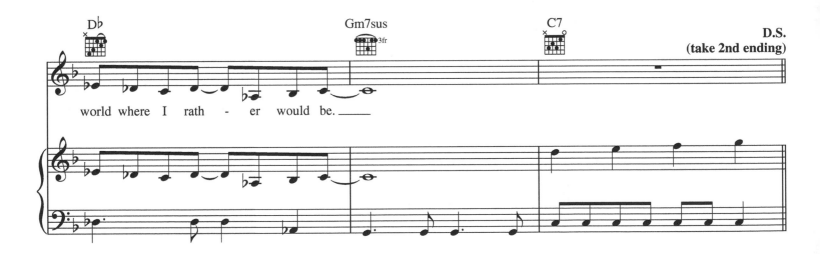

world where I rath - er would be. ___

Hon - ey, hon - ey, how ___ you thrill ___ me, a - ha, hon - ey, hon - ey.
Hon - ey, hon - ey, let ___ me feel ___ it, a - ha, hon - ey, hon - ey.

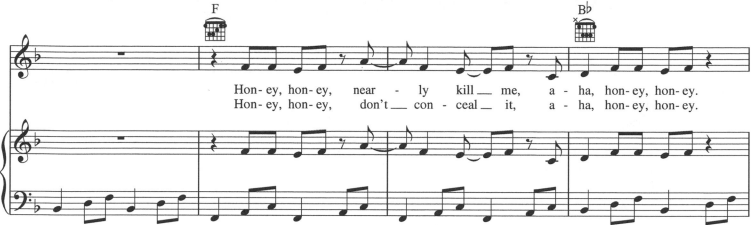

Hon-ey, hon-ey, near-ly kill __ me, a - ha, hon-ey, hon-ey.
Hon-ey, hon-ey, don't __ con-ceal it, a - ha, hon-ey, hon-ey.

I'd heard a-bout you __ be-fore, _____ I
The way that you kiss __ good-night, _____ the

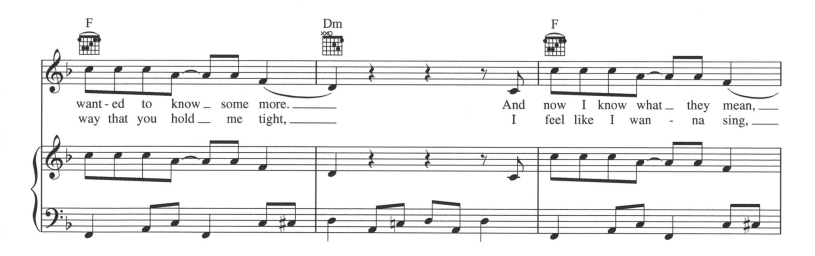

want-ed to know __ some more. _____ And now I know what __ they mean, __
way that you hold __ me tight, _____ I feel like I wan-na sing, __

Repeat and Fade

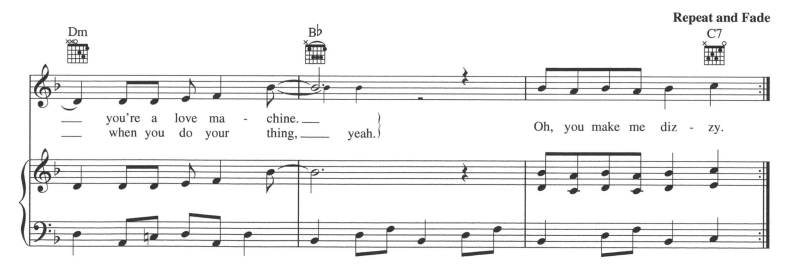

__ you're a love ma - chine. __
__ when you do your thing, __ yeah.

Oh, you make me diz - zy.

LAY ALL YOUR LOVE ON ME

Words and Music by BENNY ANDERSSON
and BJÖRN ULVAEUS

Moderately fast dance tempo

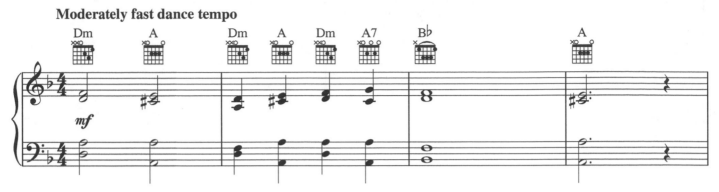

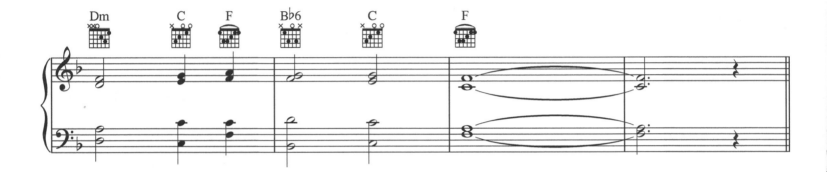

I was-n't jeal-ous be - fore we met,
It was like shoot-ing a sit-ting duck,
I've had a few lit - tle love af - fairs,

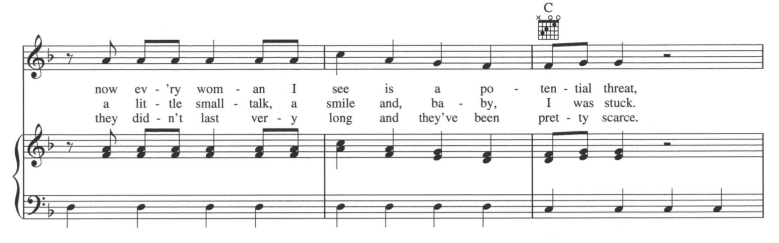

now ev - 'ry wom - an I see is a po - ten - tial threat,
a lit - tle small - talk, a smile and, ba - by, I was stuck.
they did - n't last ver - y long and they've been pret - ty scarce.

and I'm pos - ses - sive, it is - n't nice.
I still don't know what you've done with me,
I used to think that was sen - si - ble,

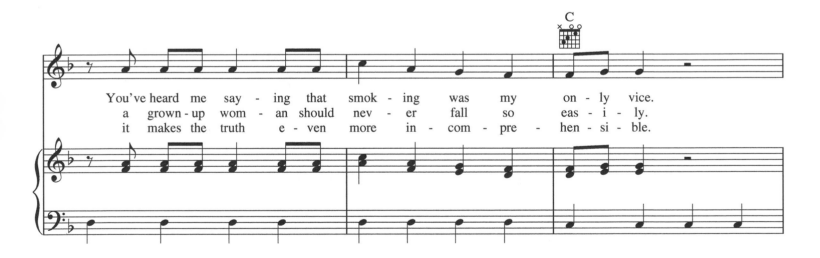

You've heard me say - ing that smok - ing was my on - ly vice.
a grown - up wom - an should nev - er fall so eas - i - ly.
it makes the truth e - ven more in - com - pre - hen - si - ble.

But now it is - n't true, ___ now
I feel a kind of fear ___ when
'Cause ev - 'ry - thing ___ is new, ___ and

ev - 'ry - thing _ is new _
I don't have _ you near, _
ev - 'ry - thing _ is you, _

and all I've learned _ has
un - sat - is - fied _ I
and all I've learned _ has

o - ver - turned. _ I beg of you: ___
skip my pride. _ I beg you, dear: ___
o - ver - turned. What can I do? ___

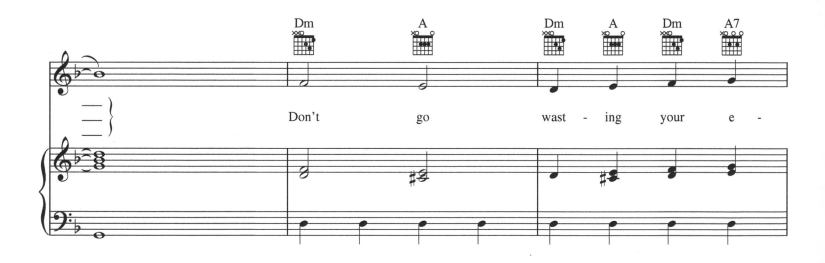

Don't go wast - ing your e -

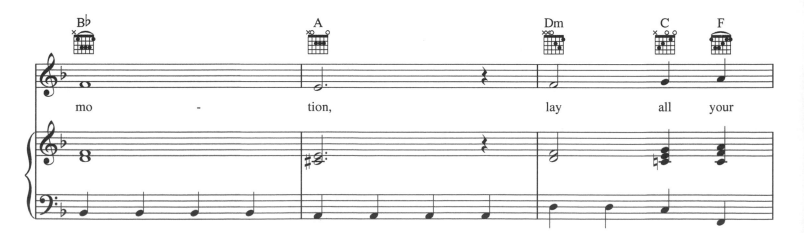

mo - tion, lay all your

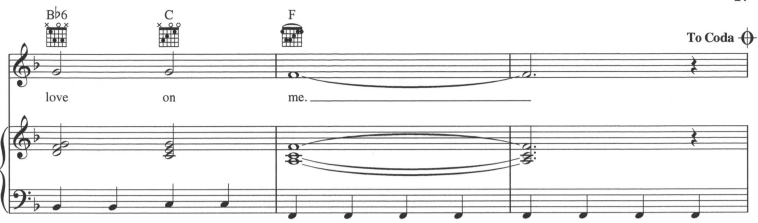

To Coda

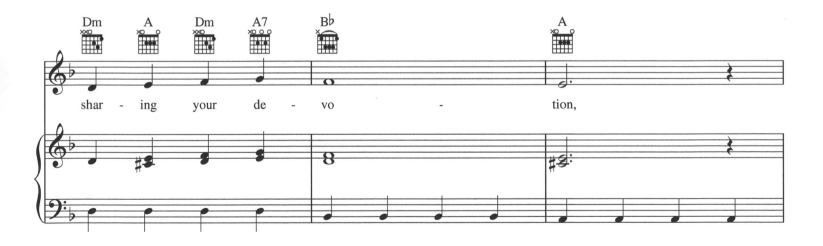

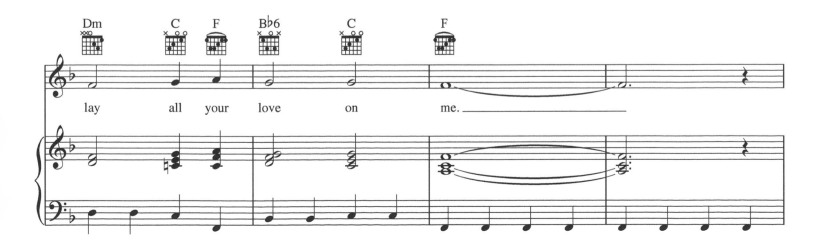

D.S. al Coda

CODA

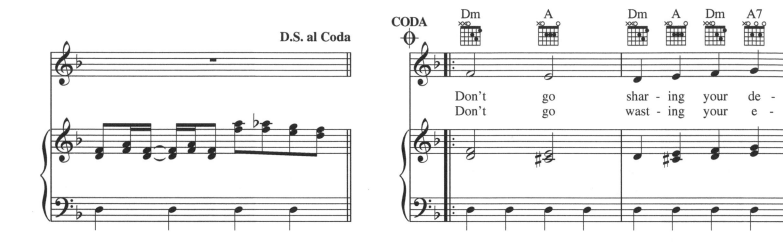

Don't go shar - ing your de -
Don't go wast - ing your e -

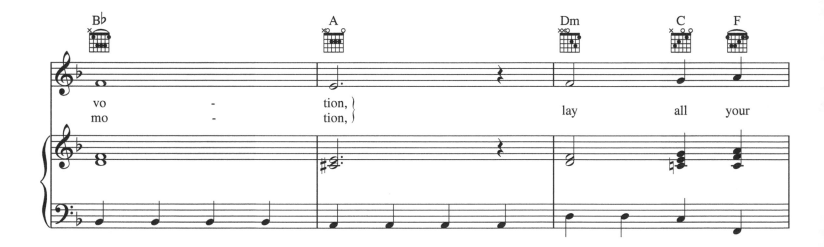

vo - tion, }
mo - tion, }

lay all your

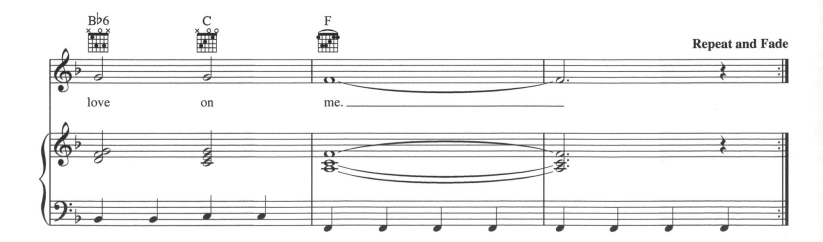

Repeat and Fade

love on me. _____

SOS

Words and Music by BENNY ANDERSSON,
BJÖRN ULVAEUS and STIG ANDERSON

Strong Rock tempo

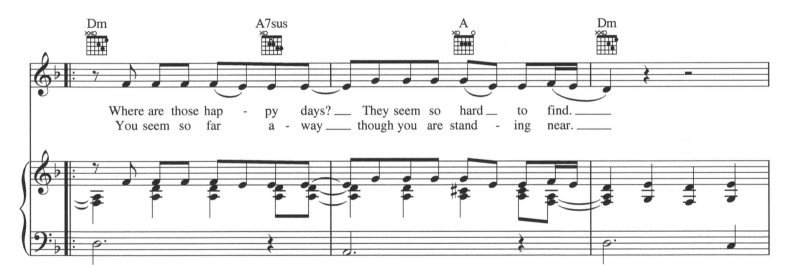

Where are those hap - py days? __ They seem so hard __ to find. ___
You seem so far a - way __ though you are stand - ing near. ___

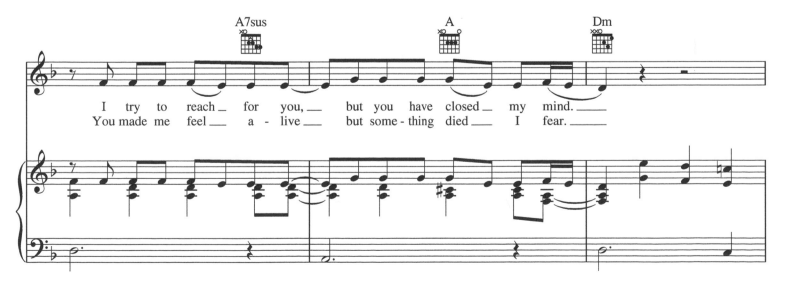

I try to reach __ for you, __ but you have closed __ my mind. ___
You made me feel __ a - live __ but some - thing died __ I fear. ___

What-ev-er hap-pened to _____ our love? I wish I un-der-stood. _
I real-ly tried to make _____ it out. I wish I un-der-stood. _

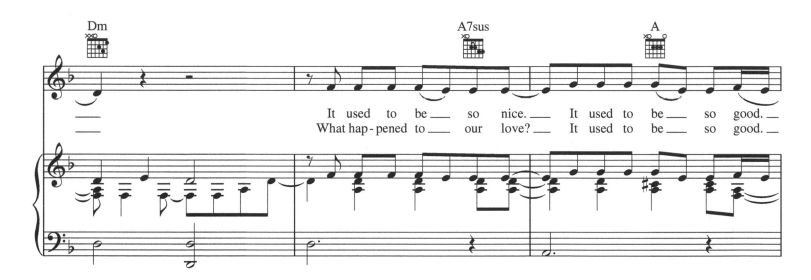

_____ so nice. _____ It used to be _____ so nice. _____ It used to be _____ so good. _____
What hap-pened to _____ our love? _____ It used to be _____ so good. _

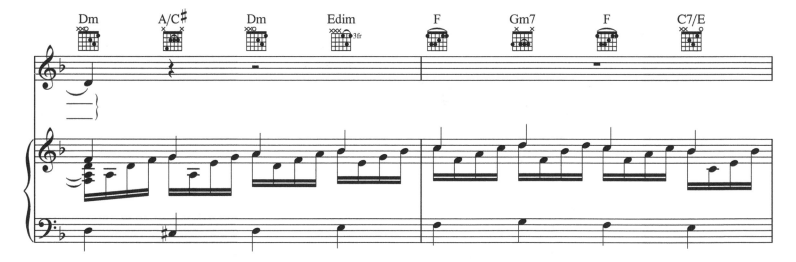

So when you're near _____ me, dar - ling, can't you hear _____ me S. _____ O. S.? _

The love you gave __ me, noth - ing else can save __ me, S. __

__ O. S. __ When you're gone, __ how can I __

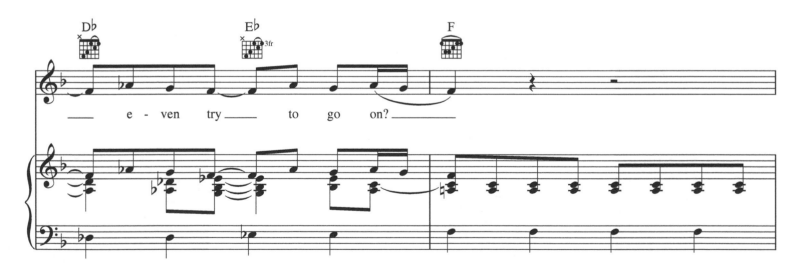

__ e - ven try __ to go on? __

When you're gone, __ though I try, __

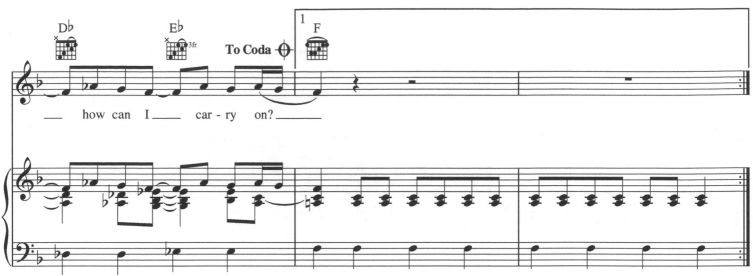

how can I car-ry on?

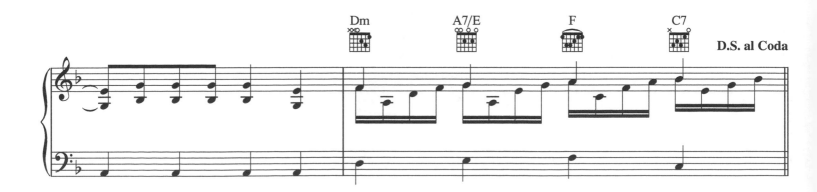

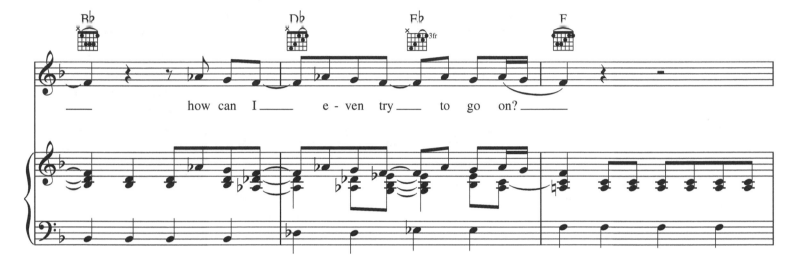

MAMMA MIA

Words and Music by BENNY ANDERSSON,
BJÖRN ULVAEUS and STIG ANDERSON

Moderately bright

N.C.

DONNA:

I was cheat-ed by you ___ and I think you know when. ___
I was an-gry and sad ___ when I knew we were through. __

So I made up my mind ___ it must come to an end. __
I can't count all the times ___ I have cried o - ver you. __

Look at me now, ___

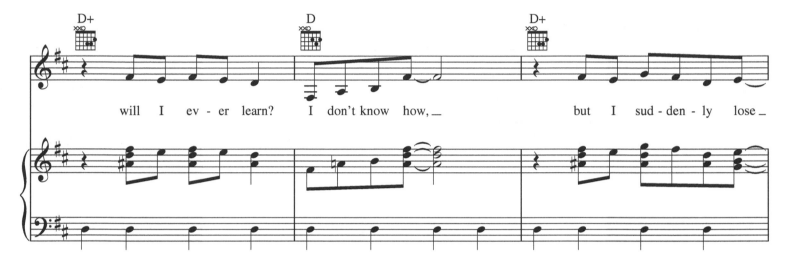

will I ev - er learn? I don't know how, ___ but I sud - den - ly lose ___

___ con - trol. ___ There's a fire ___ with - in ___ my soul. ___

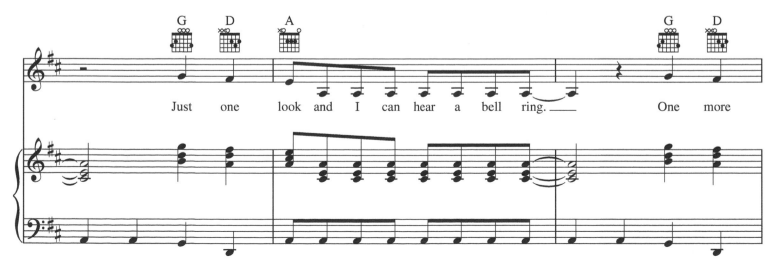

Just one look and I can hear a bell ring. ___ One more

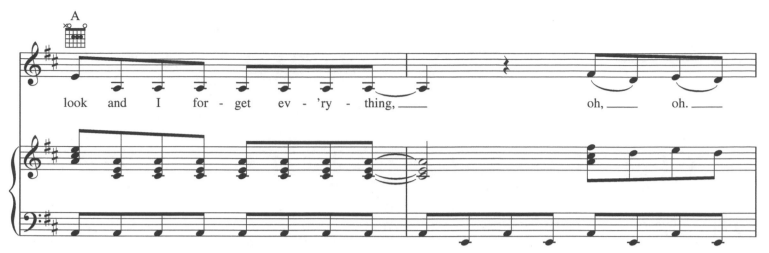

look and I for-get ev-'ry-thing, ___ oh, ___ oh. ___

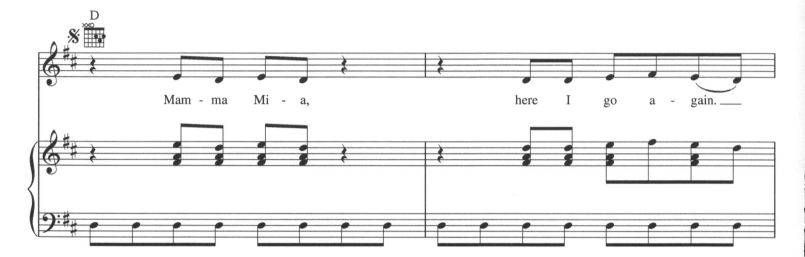

Mam-ma Mi - a, here I go a-gain. ___

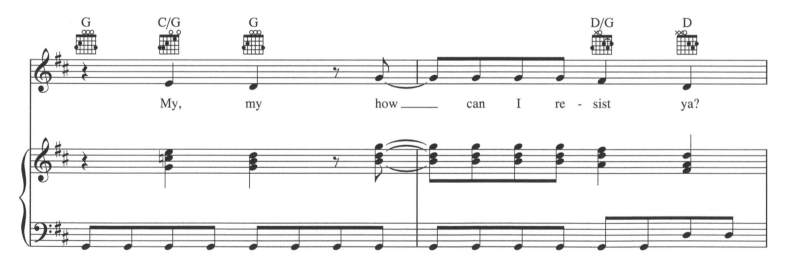

My, my how ___ can I re-sist ya?

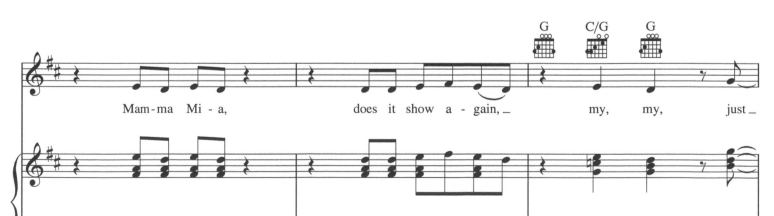

Mam-ma Mi - a, does it show a-gain, _ my, my, just _

how much I've missed ya? Yes, ___ I've been bro - ken-heart - ed,

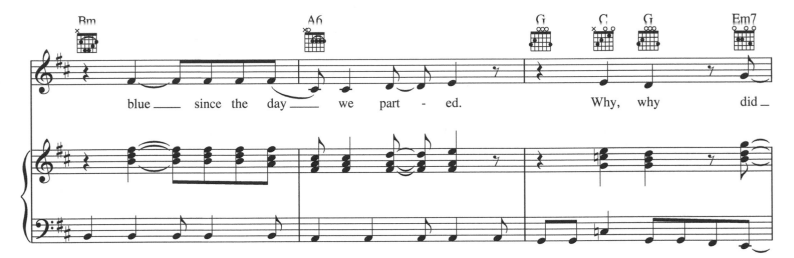

blue ___ since the day ___ we part - ed. Why, why did ___

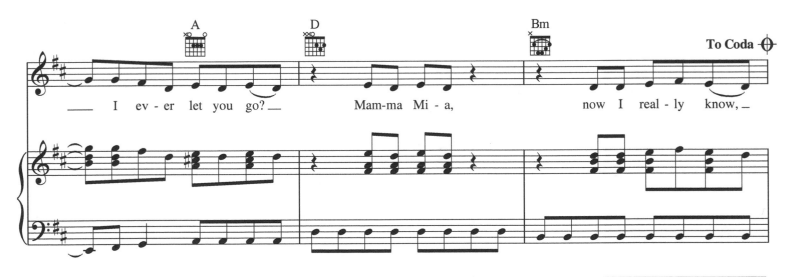

___ I ev - er let you go? ___ Mam-ma Mi - a, now I real - ly know, ___

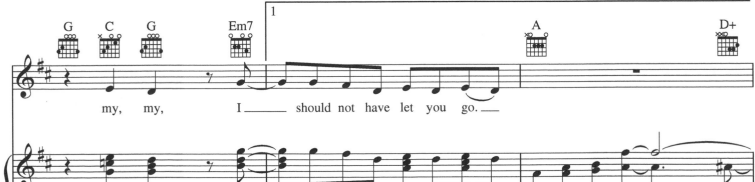

my, my, I ___ should not have let you go. ___

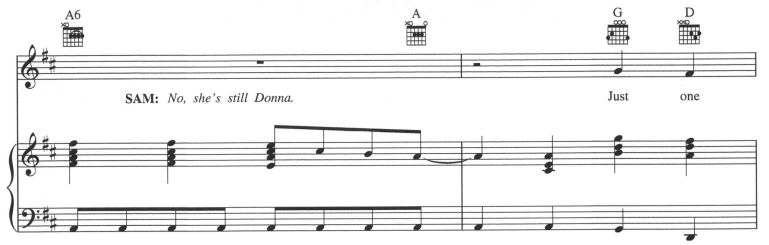

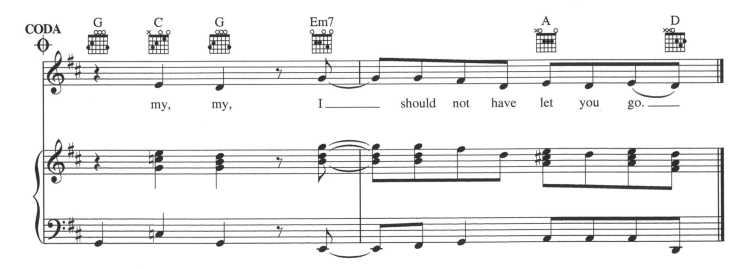

TAKE A CHANCE ON ME

Words and Music by BENNY ANDERSSON
and BJÖRN ULVAEUS

Moderate Dance beat

feel-ing down. ___ If you're all a - lone ___

___ when the pret-ty birds ___ have flown, hon-ey, I'm still free, ___

___ take a chance on me. ___ Gon-na do my ver -

- y best, and it ain't no lie, ___ if you put me to ___ the test, if you

let me try.___ Take a chance on me,_____ take a

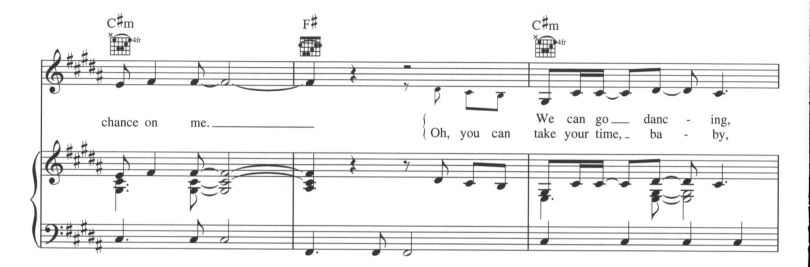

chance on me._____ (Oh, you can take your time,___ ba - by, We can go__ danc - ing,

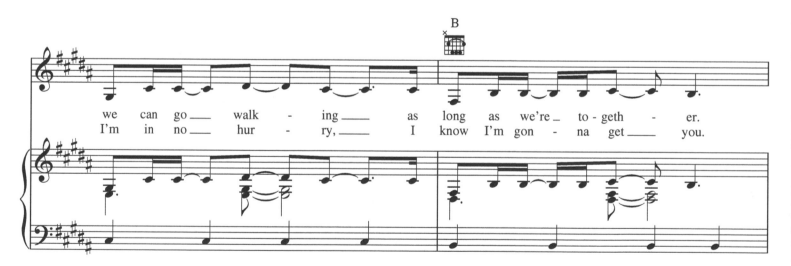

we can go__ walk - ing___ as long as we're to - geth - er.
I'm in no hur - ry,___ I know I'm gon - na get___ you.

Lis - ten to___ some mu - sic
You don't wan - na hurt___ me,

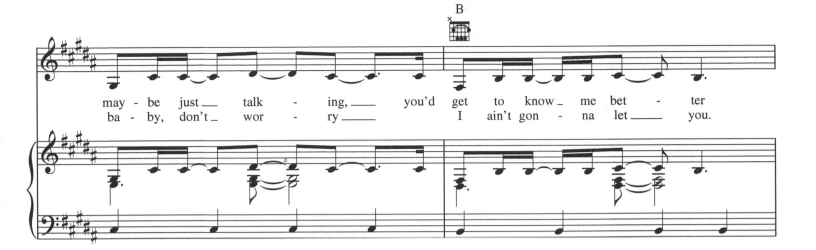

B

may - be just __ talk - ing, __ you'd get to know __ me bet - ter
ba - by, don't __ wor - ry __ I ain't gon - na let __ you.

G#m

'cause you know I got so much that I wan - na do. __
Let me tell you now my love is __ strong e - nough __

E   G#m   E   F#

When I dream I'm a - lone with you, __ it's mag - ic. __
to __ last when __ things are rough, __ it's mag - ic. __

G#m   E

You want me to leave it there, __ a - fraid of a love af - fair, __ but I
You say that I waste my time, __ but I can't get it off my mind. __ No, I

think you know ___ that I can't let go. ___
can't let go ___ 'cause I love you so. ___

If you change your mind, ___
If you change your mind, ___ I'm the first in line. ___ Hon-ey, I'm still free, ___

___ take a chance on me. ___ If you need me, let ___

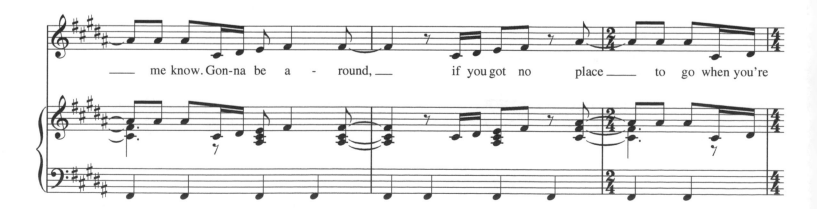

___ me know. Gon-na be a - round, ___ if you got no place ___ to go when you're

feel - ing down. ___ If you're all a - lone ___ when the pret - ty birds ___

___ have flown, hon - ey, I'm still free, ___ take a chance on me. ___

F#

___ Gon-na do my ver - y best, ba-by, can't you see, ___ got-ta put me to ___

Repeat and Fade

B

___ the test, take a chance on me. ___ If you change your mind, __

THE WINNER TAKES IT ALL

Words and Music by BENNY ANDERSSON
and BJÖRN ULVAEUS

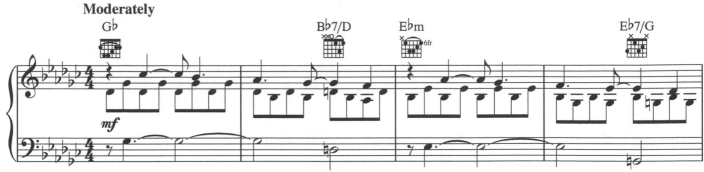

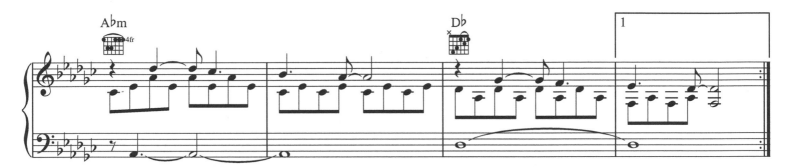

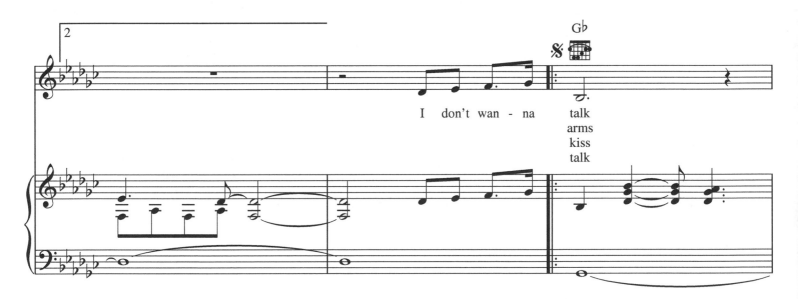

I don't wan - na talk
arms
kiss
talk

a - bout things we've gone through,
think - ing I be - longed there,
like I used to kiss you,
if it makes you feel sad,

though it's hurt - ing
I fig - ured it made
does it feel the
and I un - der -

me,
sense,
same
stand

now it's his - to - ry.
build - ing me a fence,
when she calls your name?
you've come to shake my hand.

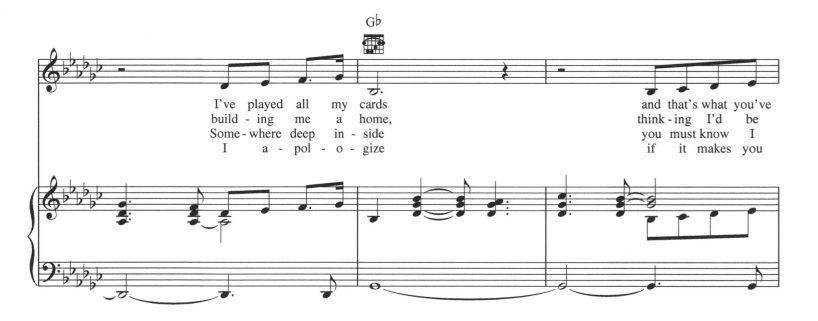

I've played all my cards
build - ing me a home,
Some - where deep in - side
I a - pol - o - gize

and that's what you've
think - ing I'd be
you must know I
if it makes you

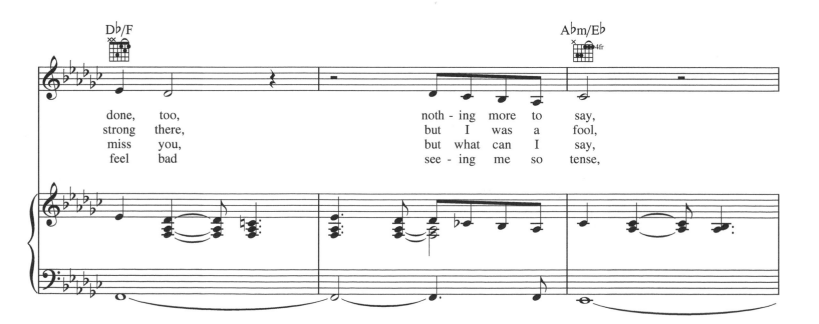

done, too,
strong there,
miss you,
feel bad

noth - ing more to say,
but I was a fool,
but what can I say,
see - ing me so tense,

42

no more ace to play.
play-ing by the rules.
rules must be o - beyed.
no self con - fi - dence.

The win - ner takes it
The gods may throw a
The judg - es will de -
The win - ner takes it

all,
dice,
cide,

the los - er stand-ing small
their minds as cold as ice,
the likes of me a - bide,

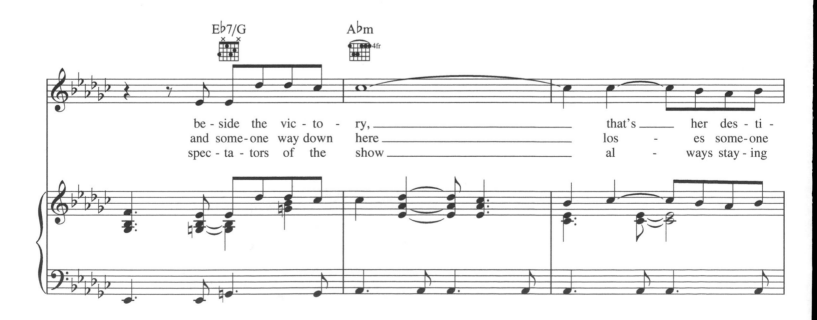

be - side the vic - to - ry, _____ that's _____ her des - ti -
and some-one way down here _____ los - es some-one
spec - ta - tors of the show _____ al - ways stay - ing

ny. _____ I was in your
dear. _____
low. _____

The win-ner takes it
The game is on a-

all,
gain,

the los-er has to fall,
a lov-er or a friend,

it's sim-ple and it's
a big thing or a

plain, _____ why should I com - plain. _____
small, _____ the win - ner takes it all. _____

D.S. al Coda

_____ But tell me, does she _____

I don't wan - na

44

Repeat and Fade

THE BEST EVER COLLECTION

ARRANGED FOR PIANO, VOICE AND GUITAR

150 OF THE MOST BEAUTIFUL SONGS EVER
00360735 150 ballads............................$32.99

BEST ACOUSTIC ROCK SONGS EVER
00310984 65 acouistic hits.....................$22.99

MORE OF THE BEST ACOUSTIC ROCK SONGS EVER
00311738 69 songs................................$19.95

BEST BIG BAND SONGS EVER
00286933 66 favorites $19.99

BEST BLUES SONGS EVER
00312874 73 blues tunes $19.99

BEST BROADWAY SONGS EVER - 6TH EDITION
00291992 85 songs................................$24.99

MORE OF THE BEST BROADWAY SONGS EVER
00311501 82 songs................................$22.95

BEST CHILDREN'S SONGS EVER
00159272 101 songs..............................$19.99

BEST CHRISTMAS SONGS EVER
00359130 69 holiday favorites...............$27.50

BEST CLASSIC ROCK SONGS EVER
00289313 64 hits.................................$24.99

THE BEST COUNTRY ROCK SONGS EVER
00118881 52 hits $19.99

THE BEST CONTEMPORARY CHRISTIAN SONGS EVER – 2ND EDITION
00311985 ....$21.99

BEST COUNTRY SONGS EVER
00359135 76 classic country hits...........$22.99

BEST DISCO SONGS EVER
00312565 50 songs................................$19.99

THE BEST DIXIELAND SONGS EVER
00312326..$19.99

BEST EARLY ROCK 'N' ROLL SONGS EVER
00310816 74 songs................................$19.95

BEST EASY LISTENING SONGS EVER
00359193 75 mellow favorites...............$22.99

BEST FOLK/POP SONGS EVER
00138299 66 hits $19.99

BEST GOSPEL SONGS EVER
00310503 80 gospel songs.....................$19.99

BEST HYMNS EVER
00310774 118 hymns $18.99

BEST JAZZ STANDARDS EVER
00311641 77 jazz hits............................$22.99

BEST LATIN SONGS EVER
00310355 67 songs................................$19.99

BEST LOVE SONGS EVER
00359198 62 favorite love songs...........$19.99

THE BEST MOVIE SONGS EVER SONGBOOK – 5TH EDITION
00291062 75 songs................................$24.99

BEST MOVIE SOUNDTRACK SONGS EVER
00146161 70 songs................................$19.99

BEST POP/ROCK SONGS EVER
00138279 50 classics $19.99

BEST PRAISE & WORSHIP SONGS EVER
00311057 80 all-time favorites...............$22.99

BEST R&B SONGS EVER
00310184 66 songs................................$19.95

BEST ROCK SONGS EVER
00490424 63 songs................................$18.95

BEST SONGS EVER
00265721 71 must-own classics $24.99

BEST SOUL SONGS EVER
00311427 70 hits $19.95

BEST STANDARDS EVER, VOL. 1 (A-L)
00359231 72 beautiful ballads...............$17.95

BEST STANDARDS EVER, VOL. 2 (M-Z)
00359232 73 songs................................$17.99

MORE OF THE BEST STANDARDS EVER – VOL. 2 (M-Z) – 2ND EDITION
00310814..$17.95

BEST WEDDING SONGS EVER
00290985 70 songs................................$24.99

HAL•LEONARD®
Visit us online
for complete songlists at
www.halleonard.com

Prices, contents and availability subject to change without notice. Not all products available outside the U.S.A.

THE ULTIMATE SONGBOOKS

Hal•Leonard® PIANO PLAY-ALONG

AUDIO ACCESS INCLUDED

These great songbooks come with our standard arrangements for piano and voice with guitar chord frames plus audio.

Each book includes either a CD or access to online recordings of full performance of each song, as well as a second track without the piano part so you can play "lead" with the band!

HAL•LEONARD®

Visit Hal Leonard Online at
www.halleonard.com

Prices, contents and availability
subject to change without notice.

PEANUTS © United Feature Syndicate, Inc.
Disney Characters and Artwork ™ © 2019 Disney

* Audio contains backing tracks only.

BIG BOOKS of Music

Arrangements for piano, voice, and guitar in books with stay-open binding, so the books lie flat without breaking the spine.

    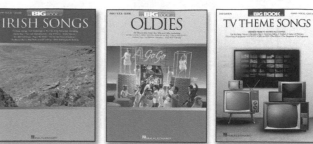

BIG BOOK OF BIG BAND HITS
84 songs: Alright, Okay, You Win • Caravan • Don't Get Around Much Anymore • I Can't Get Started with You • In the Mood • Old Devil Moon • Sentimental Journey • Star Dust • Stompin' at the Savoy • A String of Pearls • Take the "A" Train • Tuxedo Junction • more!
00310701 .... $22.99

BIG BOOK OF BLUEGRASS SONGS
70 songs: Alabama Jubilee • Blue Moon of Kentucky • Dark Holler • I Am a Man of Constant Sorrow • Mule Skinner Blues • Orange Blossom Special • Rocky Top • Wildwood Flower • and more.
00311484 .... $22.99

BIG BOOK OF BLUES
80 songs: Baby Please Don't Go • Caldonia • I'm a Man • Kansas City • Milk Cow Blues • Reconsider Baby • Wang Dang Doodle • You Shook Me • and scores more.
00311843 .... $19.99

BIG BOOK OF BROADWAY
70 songs: All I Ask of You (from *The Phantom of the Opera*) • Bali Ha'i (from *South Pacific*) • Bring Him Home (from *Les Misérables*) • Luck Be a Lady (from *Guys and Dolls*) • One (from *A Chorus Line*) • Seasons of Love (from *Rent*) • Singin' in the Rain • and more!
00311658 .... $22.99

BIG BOOK OF CHILDREN'S SONGS
55 songs: Camptown Races • (Oh, My Darling) Clementine • Do-Re-Mi • Eensy Weensy Spider • Hickory Dickory Dock • Humpty Dumpty • John Jacob Jingleheimer Schmidt • Mickey Mouse March • Pop Goes the Weasel • This Land Is Your Land • Yellow Submarine • more!
00359261 .... $17.99

BIG BOOK OF CHRISTMAS SONGS
126 songs: Away in a Manger • Carol of the Bells • Good King Wenceslas • It Came upon the Midnight Clear • Joy to the World • O Holy Night • The Twelve Days of Christmas • We Wish You a Merry Christmas • and more.
00311520 .... $22.99

BIG BOOK OF CONTEMPORARY CHRISTIAN FAVORITES
50 songs: Big House • Follow You • I Still Believe • Let Us Pray • More Beautiful You • People Need the Lord • Sing, Sing, Sing • Thy Word • What Are You Waiting For • You Reign • and many more.
00312067 .... $21.99

BIG BOOK OF '50S & '60S SWINGING SONGS
67 songs: All the Way • Blame It on the Bossa Nova • Dream Lover • I Left My Heart in San Francisco • Love and Marriage • Moonglow • That's Amore • You Belong to Me • and more.
00310982 .... $19.95

BIG BOOK OF FOLKSONGS
125 songs: Cotton Eyed Joe • Down by the Salley Gardens • Frere Jacques (Are You Sleeping?) • Hatikvah • Mexican Hat Dance • Sakura • Simple Gifts • Song of the Volga Boatman • The Water Is Wide • and many more.
00312549 .... $24.99

BIG BOOK OF FRENCH SONGS
70 songs: April in Paris • Autumn Leaves • Beyond the Sea • Can Can • I Dreamed a Dream • La Marseillaise • My Man (Mon Homme) • Sand and Sea • Un Grand Amour (More, More & More) • Where Is Your Heart • and more.
00311154 .... $22.99

BIG BOOK OF GERMAN SONGS
78 songs: Ach, Du Lieber Augustin • Ave Maria • Bist Du Bei Mir • O Tannenbaum • Pizzicato Polka • Ständchen • Vilja Lied • and dozens more!
00311816 .... $19.99

BIG BOOK OF GOSPEL SONGS
100 songs: Amazing Grace • Because He Lives • Give Me That Old Time Religion • His Eye Is on the Sparrow • I Saw the Light • My Tribute • The Old Rugged Cross • Precious Lord, Take My Hand • There Is Power in the Blood • Will the Circle Be Unbroken • and more!
00310604 .... $19.95

BIG BOOK OF HYMNS
125 songs: Blessed Assurance • For the Beauty of the Earth • Holy, Holy, Holy • It Is Well with My Soul • Just As I Am • A Mighty Fortress Is Our God • The Old Rugged Cross • What a Friend We Have in Jesus • and more.
00310510 .... $22.99

BIG BOOK OF IRISH SONGS
75 songs: Danny Boy • The Irish Washerwoman • Jug of Punch • Molly Malone • My Wild Irish Rose • Peg O' My Heart • 'Tis the Last Rose of Summer • Too-Ra-Loo-Ra-Loo-Ra (That's an Irish Lullaby) • When Irish Eyes Are Smiling • and more.
00310981 .... $19.99

BIG BOOK OF ITALIAN FAVORITES
80 songs: Carnival of Venice • Funiculi Funicula • Italian National Anthem • La Donna É Mobile • Mambo Italiano • Mona Lisa • O Mio Babbino Caro • Speak Softly, Love • Tarantella • That's Amore • and more!
00311185 .... $19.99

BIG BOOK OF JAZZ
75 songs: Autumn Leaves • Days of Wine and Roses • Falling in Love with Love • Honeysuckle Rose • I've Got You Under My Skin • My One and Only Love • Satin Doll • Take the "A" Train • The Way You Look Tonight • and more.
00311557 .... $24.99

BIG BOOK OF LATIN AMERICAN SONGS
89 songs: Always in My Heart • Feelings (Dime?) • The Girl from Ipanema • Granada • It's Impossible • La Cucaracha • Malaguena • Manha de Carnaval (A Day in the Life of a Fool) • What a Diff'rence a Day Made • and more!
00311562 .... $22.99

BIG BOOK OF LOVE SONGS
82 songs: All of Me • Endless Love • (Everything I Do) I Do It for You • Just the Way You Are • My Heart Will Go On (Love Theme from 'Titanic') • The Power of Love • Thinking Out Loud • Unchained Melody • Wonderful Tonight • You Raise Me Up • and more.
00257807 .... $22.99

BIG BOOK OF MOTOWN
84 songs: Baby Love • Get Ready • I Heard It Through the Grapevine • Just My Imagination • Lady Marmalade • My Girl • Reach Out, I'll Be There • Shop Around • Three Times a Lady • You Are the Sunshine of My Life • and more.
00311061 .... $22.99

BIG BOOK OF MOVIE MUSIC
74 songs: Beauty and the Beast • City of Stars • Eye of the Tiger • How Far I'll Go • Theme from "Jaws" • Over the Rainbow • Singin' in the Rain • Skyfall • The Sound of Music • What a Wonderful World • and more.
00260523 .... $22.99

BIG BOOK OF NOSTALGIA
158 songs: After the Ball • The Bells of St. Mary's • The Darktown Strutters' Ball • A Good Man Is Hard to Find • I'm Always Chasing Rainbows • If I Had My Way • Oh! You Beautiful Doll • Pretty Baby • Swanee • You Made Me Love You (I Didn't Want to Do It) • and more.
00310004 .... $27.50

BIG BOOK OF OLDIES
73 songs: All My Loving • Barbara Ann • Crying • (Sittin' on) The Dock of the Bay • Good Vibrations • Great Balls of Fire • Kansas City • La Bamba • Mellow Yellow • Respect • Soul Man • Twist and Shout • Windy • and more.
00310756 .... $22.99

BIG BOOK OF PRAISE & WORSHIP
52 songs: Build Your Kingdom Here • Cornerstone • Forever Reign • Lord, I Need You • One Thing Remains (Your Love Never Fails) • 10,000 Reasons (Bless the Lord) • This Is Amazing Grace • Whom Shall I Fear • and more.
00140795 .... $24.99

BIG BOOK OF ROCK
78 songs: All Right Now • Born to Be Wild • Crocodile Rock • Dust in the Wind • Fly Like an Eagle • Free Bird • Jump • Livin' on a Prayer • Paradise City • Rock and Roll All Nite • Smoke on the Water • Walk This Way • Working for the Weekend • You Really Got Me • and more.
00241569 .... $22.99

BIG BOOK OF STANDARDS
86 songs: April In Paris • Beyond the Sea • Blue Skies • Cheek to Cheek • I Left My Heart In San Francisco • Isn't It Romantic? • It's Impossible • Ol' Man River • Out Of Nowhere • Puttin' on the Ritz • Star Dust • That Old Black Magic • The Way We Were • What Now My Love • and more.
00311667 .... $19.95

BIG BOOK OF SWING
84 songs: Air Mail Special • Boogie Woogie Bugle Boy • In the Mood • Jukebox Saturday Night • Mood Indigo • Stompin' at the Savoy • A String of Pearls • Take the "A" Train • That Old Black Magic • Tuxedo Junction • and more.
00310359 .... $19.95

BIG BOOK OF TORCH SONGS
75 songs: All Alone • Bewitched • Crazy • Good Morning Heartache • Here's That Rainy Day • In a Sentimental Mood • Misty • 'Round Midnight • Stormy Weather • Too Young • and more.
00310561 .... $19.99

BIG BOOK OF TV THEME SONGS
71 songs: The Big Bang Theory • Breaking Bad • Downton Abbey • Friends • Game of Thrones • I Love Lucy • Jeopardy • M*A*S*H • NFL on Fox • The Office • The Simpsons • The Sopranos • Star Trek® • and more.
00294317 .... $22.99

BIG BOOK OF WEDDING MUSIC
77 songs: Ave Maria • Canon in D • Endless Love • In My Life • Jesu, Joy of Man's Desiring • The Lord's Prayer • Trumpet Voluntary • We've Only Just Begun • Wedding March • Wedding Processional • You Are So Beautiful • and more.
00311567 .... $22.99

Prices, contents, and availability subject to change without notice.

Visit **www.halleonard.com**
for our entire catalog and to view our complete songlists.

0121

294